洞月亮

CAVE MOON PRESS
YAKIMA 中 WASHINGTON

2017

The Body that Follows Us

The Body that Follows Us

Poems
by

Joan Swift

洞月亮

CAVE MOON PRESS

YAKIMA✝WASHINGTON

Book Design: Doug Johnson
Painting: *Infinity Dream* by Josie Gray

ISBN: 978-0692862698

Acknowledgements

Atlantic Monthly, "Light Years"
Floating Bridge Anthology,
        "Hormones," "Sand, Rose Petals, Bones"
Floating Bridge Review, "Into Ohio"
Health and Spirituality, "Roulette Rose"
Jack Straw 2006 Writers Anthology, "Jacaranda"
Many Trails to the Summit: "Magical Thinking,"
"Stillaguamish Flood"
Margie, "Blowing Out the Candles"
Poetry Northwest, "30 Degrees South Latitude" (altered somewhat),
"The Telephone Booth on Ile Royale," "Alpaca Berets," "The Migration,"
"A Patagonia Calendar Cover," "Moth"
Puerto del Sol, "Give Me"
Smartish Pace, "Geese Flying Over"
The Raven Chronicles, "The Baker on Ile Royale"
The Southern Review, "Listening to My Bones"
The Yale Review, "E", "Rainy May in the Valley," "Sixth Floor North,"
        "I Find Your Dry Fly Fishing Gear"

Section Two won the Walter Pavlich Memorial Poetry Award for a chapbook and was published by Swan Scythe Press, Sacramento, under the title *Snow on a Crocus in 2010*. My thanks for their generosity. I also owe my gratitude to the journalists at The Buffalo Evening News for their work in covering this story. And again I extend my loving thanks to Sandra McPherson and Tess Gallagher for the gifts of their time and the various wisdoms they brought to this book. Last, I am indebted to the National Endowment for the Arts for Creative Writing Fellowships and the Washington State Arts Commission for grants that helped provide the hours and inspiration needed for writing these poems.

for

Wayne and Laurie
in loving memory
and
for Lisa

Contents

Two

Three

One

Listening to My Bones

When the doctor holds my upper arm in his two hands,
he bows his head and listens as if he were waiting to hear
the song of a rare endemic bird no one has seen for centuries.
I start to speak, but he shakes his head, does not loosen his grip
on my arm, turns his fingers around the curve
of my skin and listens again.
I am afraid to clear my throat. My toes stay still.
He must hear my heart where it beats
but he is listening to the sound of bones
the way NASA turns its telescopes far over our heads on Mauna Kea
and hears the universe move.

Rain falls so hard on the roof, I think it might break through.
Imagine all those luminous drops that had been the backbone
of a cloud shattered and lying above the orthopedic surgeon's head
and mine. Soon a puddle, then a trickle into the Wailuku River.
This will mend well, he says, shows me two x-rays.
In the waiting room is a large salt water tank. A zebra moray eel
folds in one corner its brown and white stripes.
I think how it must have no bones at all
or bones so light this eel can wind
around its heaven all night when everyone has left
and dream the dream of breaking into the world.

30 Degrees South Latitude

Over the tenth deck the wild inaudible stars
are flung where you least expect them.

Standing alone in the shadow
of the ship's radar for darkness,

you see that the sky is a curving bridge
for the light steps of strangers.

They cross over alone or in groups
and the next night cross silently over

again without saying where
they have been or why they are

doomed to repeat the same journey.

You open your book of constellations,
think how somebody wanted this sky

to be home like earth—
mountain, dove, scorpion, river, wolf.

When the bear you've known since you were a child

hangs on the horizon's lowest limb
you capture it there with your eyes, desiring

the known even though it pours its own
black blood into black.

Light Years

Is light the last thing lost or never lost at all?
There is light so far away, it's gone

by the time we see it,
the tail lights on the highway far ahead

that say someone is traveling
this same dark way.

Those blue clumps lost ten billion light
years ago at the edge of the universe

redshift from ultraviolet to the visible
and are found by the Hubble telescope,

sleek horse pulling through dark
the reeling carriages of space

even as they change into roses
or thunderheads or phantom animals

we never imagined.
What fiery dust was our beginning,

left us a tender earth? Far out in the universe
a tomorrow we can't see is singing the last word

of a song we heard long ago under stars
like blossoms on black water.

E

floats slantwise down the eye chart,
almost becomes an M before
in the pool of the vitreous
it changes to a child's way of writing.
Then, a little off center on the retina
it slides into the optic nerve upside down,
assuming at the utterly last instant

the guise of a W. O
it dives into the conscious
like a circus performer,
no different than the rest of the alphabet
so that if we could see the wild turns,

we'd have the word MEW,
language of the cat curled on your chest.
But we are a higher species
and must pull out the net in our brain
where the letter lands
so it can somersault off to be E again.
You're sprawled on the sofa

head on my pillows the color of grass
in a meadow, your breakfast grapefruit, the vein
on the back of your hand that rivers
blood back from the brain. You're
reading a book, oblivious to the performance

the whole world passing through the crystalline
lens of your eye turned
upside down. To have to set the pale
pink petals of the rhododendron
upright on their stems again
or the golf green on TV
back down where it belongs

it's no wonder we're weary every night.
Yet you lounge there half asleep
while the universe is captured,
flipped over like birch trees reflected in still
water, needing to assume its original shape.

But if I forget the black holes out there
in unreadable space
already the reverse of everything,
a bevy of alter worlds lurking among the stars
where even the slowly swirling E collides
among its many selves falling through time
along with everything we've ever loved—

the moon, delphinium,
the child, the grace of rain—
it's because you turn a page, look up,
and say you love the sky when it's this clear,
this cloudless blue.

Astronomy

Our daughter wants a diamond ring pierced
through the cusp of her navel.
She talks on her cell phone with friends
about possible pain, antiseptics, how many
days of recovery, choosing a piercer.

The jewel will gleam over her thong,
shine in her belly button, light up her bikini
like a marquee. While she sleeps
it will nestle in her tummy fold, flake
of a gem glinting where we once were moored.

Tonight I look toward the sea and above,
in the sky, night's slender girl
drifts as if hypnotized toward conjunction
with a star of the first magnitude.
My moom, she used to call it,

rising above the mountains.
While I held her on the hood of the car
so she saw better the only body that follows us,
she was dreaming how she might place
in the curve of herself such light.

Stillaguamish Flood

This is where we drank champagne for your ninetieth
birthday. Slowly below the river sorted its way
over the same old stones, braided the several blues
it kept using over and over. The cabin was new,
smelled of fresh cedar, the peak of its roof high
in firs. All the rhododendrons you'd planted
were heavy with purple, magenta, that deep shade
of pink seen only at dawn or at sunset.

This is where you cut me a walking stick
when I stopped by with the dog,
when I stepped into the water to follow
a man from Fisheries counting the nests of salmon.
Maples were spilling their rust and yellow,
scattering scraps on a small red swing you hung
from a lowest branch. Leaves turned and turned
in the slow fall currents of the Stillaguamish.

This is where I came to write one snowy winter
when the river was gray and eagles dove for dead salmon
and I was too cold for words. They won't come now
even in benediction, even goodbye, goodbye
and see you later to the boards of the cabin
never found when the flood receded, not a spoon
or a saucer, not the cup I would lift to transcience
and pour out the river that stays and stays.

Ferns in June

They swim for their lives,
throwing their fronds over
the waves of air—
lady fern, licorice fern,
sword fern, maidenhair.
They race one another across
channels of sun,
wind straits, bays of deep shadow
under the cedars and firs
that root for them
in subterranean voices.
They have already uncurled
the small fists
they used to break through the earth
and dive past the surf of salal
where it crashes on huckleberry.
No one can tell them
they will be buried for eons again
inside a black planet.
If I open the window
they will plunge over the sill.
They will take me in their arms.

Rainy May in the Valley

This is the warp of the loom as it escapes
through the farmhouse window, leaves
the factory behind, slides out the door

of the homely craftswoman who wants to
sell her art at the fair. The threads have
turned silver from traveling so long in the sky

but the shuttle hangs onto its reason,
throws a blanket over Whitehorse
woven of heavy meanderings, scraps

caught from the river, strands of the ocean
spun to such thick visibility
the mountain vanishes altogether.

Outside the window, the native species
rise into fabric they love,
cedars and Douglas firs, Pacific dogwood

unfolding white umbrellas inside out.
Each one cups the small drink
it will need later on, after the rain

that wraps all of us now has been sewn
into the web of a spider, glisten of moisture
connecting one branch to another.

Moth

All night I lay under the spread
of its wings
the scales falling gently, invisibly
silver and that shade of tan
that can suddenly seem gold
or drift back to silver
as I sleep and in the morning
it is always wherever moths go in daylight.

Imagine being invertebrate
and stretching your wings fully
against your own invented sky,
latitude and longitude vanished
the same as they disappear in the universe
and you are the only galaxy
weaving your stripes and spots
across space longing for light.

Those upward spirals
under the shade of the bedroom lamp,
those kamikaze dives for the bulb
require no war
or passport only
some emergence from a darkness
you wove around yourself.
They say you navigate by keeping
the moon on a horizontal.
Who flew first—a bird or you?

With what wisdom did you put on
your capes of dun brocade
to go hunting along
the gray bark of the maple
with those thousands of others?
You fold into each other like Japanese
fans held silently
against the breasts of a woman.
I have never once heard your cry.

Poncho

Because laying the fabric
down on the wet sand
will send it away to its final sleep

because the sea is deep enough
for these sky blue stripes on the sleeves
and the raspberry huckleberry swath

of the cloth that once wrapped me,
I let the waves come up to the silver fringe
and yearn for its drowning

this garment I wore on a cruise ship,
and when it was new with purple tights
to a Christmas party

and then on this same yellow sand
where it starts even now to fill
with the wind of the surf.

The sea moves like the shuttle under the hand
weaving the cloth that covered him—
you know the photograph—

his bare feet on a box at Abu Graib,
black hood over his head,
arms a supplicant's.

wires hanging from his fingers
so he thinks two thousand volts will kill him
if he falls from his narrow perch—

black bird, slim prisoner, some
weeping woman's husband, hustler,
thief, lost boy.

He wears a poncho just like mine,
the pattern many roses climbing
the trellis of his terror.

The Pacific pulls my poncho out to sea.
The one he wore waiting for death in the dark
belongs to all of us.

Shin-Ichi's Tricycle

I stepped down from the trolley that day in Hiroshima
and walked by the river where the children had floated in flames,
but I could not hear their cries of *misu, misu.* Lost.

I saw the rowboats tied to the shore waiting for the living,
and the Prefecture building as the autumn wind
blew through the skeletal dome and every leaf lay scattered.

I passed by heaps of flowers and burning candles
to the doors that let me in to where the lights were dim,
so many shadows, each display lit only by a row of flashlights.

Power outage, someone said and so I need not pay my yen
but paid another way past fingers dripping skin,
a lunch box full of barley ash, the twisted tricycle

Shin-Ichi's mother dug from severed earth. She gave it
so the boy would live in memory:
sculptured handlebars and pedals burned to black

all buried by the father who found him lying dead.
I thought of myself at five,
pedaling my tricycle down the middle

of Wilsonia Road, the rainbow shine of oil,
the sun, my father's call
as he came swooping down to pull me back,

shouting, Don't ever do that again.
Although of course I would.
And of course we did.

About Guns

We were at Bill's farm and I was about thirteen
looking at the tin can Bill set on a stump
for a target near the apple orchard.

Mother wasn't shooting the rifle, just watching Bill
as she wondered about the deer that might wander down among
the fallen apples, their delicate hooves

picking among the stones. She'd already given herself
to one ungentle ending so I could tell that thought,
even as she turned her gaze to the river running

shallow and clear below, on its way to the Susquehanna
and then to Chesapeake Bay, and then to other water
that would become an ocean.

I held the rifle to my shoulder and looked through the sight,
trying to keep in mind what Bill said about the kick.
then pulled the trigger. The shot echoed away

into the hazy end-of-summer sky, part gray, part blue,
with a white sliver of moon like a fishbone
cast aside but still remembering the same old migration route.

And there was a bullet that flew off with that sound—
I don't want to forget that although I'll never know
where it buried itself.

I wasn't thinking about the ocean or the war beginning
on the other side. Nor of the class in solid geometry
ahead of me, where my favorite boys all left to learn

that a gun sight was a new set of lines crossing lines
with death in the middle of some country
whose language is written in blood,

language that told them to lie still on the sand
or the vines of a jungle or under the tree
whose fruit in the story was forbidden.

Sometimes, although loving what lived, Bill shot pheasant,
iridescent innocents of grass and air
and lay them warm on the kitchen counter for my mother.

Sixth Floor North

The lost second makes only
the smallest sound. Like a nomad it wanders
all night the desert of the hospital room,
having by mistake dropped out of the clock
the nurse cradled down from its hook
because I asked for no time.
                              If a second
is like the ripped stitch
in the weave of a camel's hair sweater,
then all other seconds are this minute slowly
unraveling past the space of the window
in search of where in the world
they might fit anymore.
                          Or if a second
is one drop of a whole ocean into whose blue
it always flies back…
                    But here
some Bedouin passes with the promise

of dawn across his burnoose;
on the windowsill where he pauses,
Skagit Valley tulips, a visitor's gift, doubling
and redoubling their blood red in the dark.

The Cousins Talk About Osteoporosis

1.

If we break a hip we'll die, our doctors warn.
Across their desks they push box after box of
Actonel, Fosamax, Calcitonin Salmon,
calcium pills with enough vitamin D to prove
the sun unnecessary if we didn't, of course,
love it just for the way it turns the sky blue
and the sea into an endless floating carpet of diamonds.
Exercise! they say, or our bones will go up the flue—
departing ghosts—and unlike those blondes
who can't be too thin, bones hide their brittleness.
Take in your hands the weight of a dumbbell
and pretend it's a feather fallen from a bird,
a bird whose bones are slender, light, and shell-
like, although the bird flies under a heavy cloud.

2.

And then there is the genetic factor.
Off the southwest coast of County Cork, storms
pounding the cliffs rode into our bones with their
rain of dissolution. Sad chromosomes
gathered on the stem—we were still mere shadows
of the unborn. How our great-grandmother brought
among her petticoats and shawls and buttoned shoes
our future over the ocean is what we talk about
on Sunday afternoons from coast to coast.

But doesn't earth call bones the most
beloved part of the body, show its care
by keeping them in its own depth forever—
ribs and femurs, skulls in a meadow's loam
after the journey, after the long dream.

Nepal, 1990

We go to the shore to see the sun
paint all the Annapurnas
rhododendron peach and orange and flame

while a mile away the kohl-eyed queen
in hiding at the summer palace
orders her servant to play the Hindu

dawn music on the loudspeaker.
She knows the revolution is small but real.
As we step into the boat,

the lake rocks in the little wind
that sometimes blows over the edge of a teacup.
Would it be fate then to say

we drift for a moment
on the watery silks of history?
I want to see the shadow that falls

over the queen's face, the king eating
his breakfast mango,
the small aunts in their red saris,

the princes home from Eton on a holiday,
especially in my binoculars
the prince who eleven years from now

will kill them all. For love.
A guard makes a mark in the waves
where destiny says we shall not pass.

For love he will kill them all and then himself—
forbidden lost still yearning heart's desire—
while, you and I, old oar, will years ago

have turned the water over, watched the drops
break our reflections, then the circles
that go on forever start their journey.

Alpaca Berets

The merchants on San Angelmo in Puerto Montt
arrange dozens of small alpaca berets into towers
of the purest haloes, black or brown or gray,
the animal's color before its hair ever became a halo,
and invite me to try them on.

Each stall with berets in concentric
circles, as if a cook had prepared too
many pancakes, is available to anyone
who walks in from the cracked sidewalk.
In some of the stalls, sausages hang from a beam.
Tomatoes and pears shine in Chile's morning sun.

I try on a halo.
Nine hundred pesos, the merchant says
and I'm sold at two dollars American,
worth it for perching on my head
an eternity of such texture.
Neruda adored the wool of his socks
and the socks even more because
of the fingers that knit and offered them.

I save this beret for someone who knows
nothing yet of the Southern Hemisphere,
that there is such a thing and also many oceans,
unaware of the Andes where the alpaca
who gave its hair still grazes,
a fresh coat of down beginning
on its skin and shining.

The Telephone Booth on Ile Royale

They come up to the booth like children
with empty bowls—the Filipino wine steward
a cabin boy from Sukarta.

They approach with the caution of white-tailed deer,
take a step or two back before entering
to read the instructions: the image of a telephone,

a mouth open as in speaking, the silent
half circles which are the words growing out
toward the swallowing sea

where they want their voices to flow.
Given half the afternoon off, they are
the last to arrive by the ship's tender.

They wear the insouciant off-duty clothes
of their countries, the loose cotton
of an emergency ward.

Now they seem at a loss on the still lawn,
turn away from the booth under coconut palms,
its graffiti in all the unknowable languages,

its demand for francs and credit cards.
away from the path to the crumbling prison.
Near the small boat launch, not there

when inmates ate cockroaches for protein,
the leatherback turtles rise for air
in the equatorial stillness of the island.

they who have never tasted
blood
or been lonely.

The Baker on Ile Royale

Dry yeast and flour on last night's ship
from the mainland. The inmate carried
the burlap sack tenderly. *Faim.*
Il ne pense qu'a de faim.
He will not be eating what I bake.

Now dawn and the kettle steams
with it precious cargo of water.
Three-quarters of a cup, two
and two-thirds of a cup.

Rain gave it. A tree in burgundy gave
its heartwood to the spoon
whose *whup whup* is the morning's only song.
Sugar, salt, butter from the work camp.

I have a gift for bread. I sway,
kneading the dough as if I were rocking a boat,
digging the heels of my hands in,
pushing the dough away

as I would shove a boat from the shore
of the island to escape, robber of banks,
rapist, whatever I am.

Sometimes I think I smell cinnamon,
garlic, cardamom,
tongue angels from home.

Sometimes I bite into the crust of a loaf
Before I deliver it to the warden.

Voices

On the whale-watching catamaran out of Maalaea
when the naturalist shouts *flukes at two o'clock,*
we all rush to starboard like a tsunami.

He lures us back with a spout at nine.
When a whale breaches, the whole Pacific Ocean slides
down its back as if many hands plaited water.

The females want a minute alone to slide naked
in their skins through warm water, to spill milk
into the mouths of their calves where they suck near vaginal slits.

But the males want to sing. They can't help it.
The songs are a million years old, maybe older.
You can hear them with your ears in the ocean.

Once you gave me two sterling silver humpback whales,
earrings I worry I might put on backwards by mistake
just as the whales may forget in what direction to swim

when they hear the roar of sonar in the sea,
they who have always known where voices come from
and where in the deepest dark they are going.

All of us have heard voices.
Sometimes we turn and we find the one who speaks to us,
sometimes the room is empty.

Jacaranda

Imagine ascending
into the February
branches of the jacaranda
just now beginning to open
its blossoms
near the edge of
the Mamalahoa Highway
and like a woman fallen
in love stretching out
between the old life and the new
with your hair streaming
and your arms folding
and your legs drifting
onto a bed of blue feathers,
blue cumulus,
blue butterflies
while the world goes north
and the world goes south below
where you dream,
only the curve of your cheek visible—

Give Me

Rain is falling on the skylight
even as the moon drops in

wearing its silk parachute
the color of clouds.

There is the strangeness of white hibiscus
floating down from the black sky

and a sense the drowning must have,
that in darkness they are brighter than water

like the unborn not yet laid on a mother's breast,
both wet and radiant.

She might be dead somewhere, I think,
and I would never know

what pill, which artery,
how quietly the drops of blood...

She had no hair for tying the nursery ribbon to,
little fuzz on a dewberry.

The wind plays with this rain,
no way to prophesy direction.

I wad the sheet in a damp ball under my chin.
Only the moon knows where it's going.

The Migration

Because I am imagining inside
one of the brain's dimly-lit lobes where
draperies crinkle and wrap over the shape
of my thought, although they think
I am down in the brain stem
where muscles have minions
and lungs need to be told to take in
the hospital air...

because I see rain falling and remember
the Magellanic penguins of Punta Arenas,
the distances they swim in the Cape Horn
Current, never wondering when
to head in for shore, always knowing
where the grass blows yellow,
I cannot separate myself to look
from any other window.

Although they think it is death,
it is only a path I follow among hummocks.
It is only a burrow I line with my own down.

Technology

All the cell phone towers are pagodas
from the top floor through my near-sighted eyes—
blue, white, red shimmering houses
for ancient gods among the fir trees and dogwood.
They climb the hills to the cemetery, carrying
the voices of the living far above the lost
chatter of those already gone before us.

The words are like raindrops in a summer storm
here then gone, sadness borne away
over the continents. And love
or the failure of love, wounds and caresses.
The seas wander underneath.
Somewhere in this forest of voices
a pen is writing in blue ink.

Geese Flying Over

The geese were flying south over our heads,
calling compass points and wind sheer.
Rain fell hard on all of us, the clouds above
sharing their own way of staying in touch.

I was running from the parked car
to your house. So were you.
The geese flew in the wild formation they invented:
many wings, like origami, folding to one known place.

I remember dogs were barking at the geese.
All across the driveway leaves of your ornamental pear
lay in drifts of red, blood red, and wine.
You had recently lost your husband to a heart attack.

Then suddenly the geese were gone.
The sky dropped low above us.
Time for lamplight on your husband's
collection of wooden lures for fishing

through ice. They swam across the table,
the shine of their paint that spoke to other fish.
We sipped Ethiopian coffee.
I imagined the geese falling asleep among tules

and that weathered artifact outside your door
he bought you at a county fair, black
paint chipped and claws still hanging on,
saying to the mist, "Two old crows live here."

For Theodore Roethke

The poet who was my teacher said we must rewrite.
It was a warm afternoon. Sun dabbled in the greenhouse.
So now I revise and revise until I think the real writing
is rewriting. First drafts are small forays into the hills
from which I bring back a pail half full of unripe
blueberries that may, on closer look, be
some other kind of fruit entirely. I remember
he leaned back in the chair and waved his hand
and said my poem describing salmon was really about sex.

*

We stood facing the faded paint of Parrington's walls
each Friday, memorizing lines of a poem we chose to recite—
to learn the sound of the words together and the little spaces
between the sounds.   Each of us quaked.
Inside the classroom he turned to the ravishing co-ed on his right,
the one with the throaty voice and said,
Play that for us on your bazooka, will you, honey?
She nearly fainted but she spoke the lines.
No one has ever made Louise Bogan sound like that.

*

He brought a straw hand basket belonging to his wife.
It was stuffed with books. "She'll kill me, " he said,
heaving it down on the table, the one who taught him
Turn and Counter-Turn and Stand, who taught him Touch,

that undulant white skin. We leaned to see what rivers
might pour forth, what three-beat lines, what metaphysical
poets hidden between the spines, what rose, what sorrow.
Later, in my car beneath the flagpole, he said to kiss him on his cheek just
once. In the rearview mirror, there she was.

*

Who, sitting in the tea house, doesn't know he died too soon?
Beyond the posts and beams, a roof of glass.
the swimming pool is sculptured sand. Five rocks
(the five-beat line?) mark where his breath last sighed
to any bird: the anniversary of his death day.
The last thing he said to me was,
There's going to be a special graduate class next fall
and you're in it. Years passed and one by one
we learned he said that to all of us.

Roulette Rose

How do I have the luck to choose by chance
from the chilled glass case this rose, of all things, called Roulette?

After they tested you alive to see how dead the dreadful cells were,
you bring a bottle of wine named "Working Girl Red"

and we drink a toast to you at the kitchen counter. What luck
did you look for when you married him in the Heart of Reno Chapel

then played roulette at Harrah's? You knew
he'd never live to see leaves tumble across the grass

like dice in craps, that loosening of the fingers
giving over to the not-yet-known.

You acknowledge the day each year. Sometimes you ride a black horse
to his grave as wind from the strait ripples your new hair.

In the morning, coffee stirs up talk and a small bird hops in a pine.
When you drive away the rose lies waiting in the dark refrigerator.

There's a moment then when I send a husband off to chase
the wish of laying that rose on another's husband's grave.

Already the bud has suddenly flared open, already is starting to droop,

So when the ferry leaves its own white blossom on the water, nothing's
        lost.

Now here is the girl at the flower counter telling me
never to place roses close to oranges, lemons, limes.

A rose wants to be near the bakery.
Bread of life.

For Tess

Two

I pull my coat around me…I rock and lament my foolish ways,
but even if I had been wise I would have failed to change my fate;
Lament my foolishness then and later and now, for which I would like so much to
be forgiven.

Czeslaw Milosz
New and Collected Poems
1931-2001

Hundreds of neonaticides occur each year…
Societal institutions and the professionals who
who run them have failed to acknowledge the patterned
nature of this phenomenon, and have sought
instead to haphazardly blame such crimes solely
on the individuals who commit them.

Cheryl L. Meyer and Michelle Oberman
Mothers Who Kill Their Children

The Start of the Story and Some of the End

You walk through waterfalls all afternoon
and rainbows made of the drenched sun.

There is enchantment
where you step through yarrow, aster, mint.

A spell falls over you and love
is nothing else but lying down, a dove

on each of your bare toes and on his back
a tee shirt you keep pulling on like

a bell for all the ringing. Later
snow will fall on your mother's hair

as she walks from her car to the courtroom.
Killing is always the same.

The child will circle your days long after she's gone
like a boat that swings on an anchor chain

and never heads out to sea
day after trembling day.

Journey

You know his baby is inside you when you smell the French fries
he passes from the frozen custard stand right under your nose.

He has the lake's grace—the rough and shove of a wind-blown
    wave
and the transparent running of water up the shore's concave

bowl of sand. Your stomach lurches but you don't let him know
when he hands you a hot dog through the car window,

your black running back making this touchdown.
Woman in love on a late summer afternoon,

you pull your fingers through strands of your light hair
and try not to tell him a baby is there

suddenly between you. Exiled Pacific salmon are just begin-
ing their run from the lake, scales that could be sun

on the small creek's surface or leaves blowing over, copper, bronze,
the reds and golds that drift around and through a salmon's

collective memory, fish transplanted from the other side of the land
to this distance of strange water. There's a bend

in the stream where they remember the rush
to the sweetness of milt over eggs although there's death in that
    push

to staying alive. Now you lean on his shoulder
like a child about to cry, trying to think how and where

and when to quietly
begin your journey.

Magical Thinking

You talk to yourself these days about yourself:
There is no baby here inside me.
Listen to me, walls, blue bed, white pages
of this chemistry book that tells no lies,

the sun flies down and lights on me alone.
I talk to myself these days about myself
because there's no one else
to listen to me. Walls, blue bed, white pages

on the desk beside the open window
where the sun flies down and lights on me alone,
soothe me in my sorrow, in my knowing
that there's no one else.

I have a lover. He says we're growing cells
near the desk beside the open window
where I sit, reading *Paradiso, The Inferno*.
(Soothe me in my sorrow, in my knowing.)

It's not here, not in this world, I say,
although my lover says we're growing cells.
He says you're crazy, baby. Just get real.
I'm reading *Paradiso, The Inferno*.

If it's a hundred yesterdays ago today
it won't be there, not in this world, I say.
The first flower can wither in the frost.
He says you're crazy, baby. Just get real.

Listen to me, walls, blue bed, white pages.
These days I'm talking to myself about myself.

Into Ohio

Dry leaves blow across the road and scatter—
small animals running into the brittle grass—
and you lie down in the back seat of the car,
you lie and watch your lover's hooded face
in profile as he drives. You want to yell
at him again. He wants to hit you, hold you
down by both arms. This is not a fairy tale
where babies drift to shore in a canoe.

In the morning the doctor at the clinic
says it's way too late, he'd have to do a partial
birth abortion, drive through the brain a pick
and he won't. You see on the sonogram a girl
as she comes swirling up in the light of her bones,
waiting for the world's love, though she waits alone.

Christmas Night

God is in his house among the stars
so to God you cannot speak,
and your mother is cleaning up the leftovers.

Finding grace in the boughs of the dark
fir tree will not happen. You must go up step by step
to your bedroom, gather your blankets and a book.

Ponder the small life inside you with her occasional hiccup.
Whether to cross into the country of the blessed
and keep her—rattles, bells—or, lacking a map

of the dun plains, wander alone with the lost.
There is still time before the bud breaks from its caul,
to save you both, to choose what is most

honest and simple. Downstairs the dishes rattle
in the dishwasher. Under your ribs the child's dance
is a samba. And now your mother comes and you can tell

her, you can help yourself to this glittering chance
wheeling just out of reach. When she asks you
Honey, are you pregnant? the irretrievable nonce

hangs in the air like a single flake of snow
you could catch on your tongue.
And you say *No.*

Sweater Villanelle

You think how good it is to be pregnant in winter,
since you're pregnant. You throw
a big woolly sweater, the one you call My Bear,

over your bulging belly as your drive the car
through a blizzard, the wild light-headedness of snow.
You think how good is it to be pregnant in winter

with all these flakes falling around you like the pure
covering of some religion. Are you cold with what you know
inside your woolly sweater? Can you bear

the knowing? A scarf hangs loosely from your shoulder
to conceal your engorged breasts. They hurt. The two
of you think how good it is to be pregnant in winter

so no one will guess: a down jacket or Gortex outerwear
disguising the baby. You don't know yet how
in your big woolly sweater you will have to bear

down as your body lights up with a fire,
how the baby will drop so small and so blue
onto the tile floor in the hardness of winter,
how your big bloody sweater will hide what's bare.

Blowing Out the Candles

Snow falls like feathers outside the dorm window.
Breast feathers of towhees, feathers of snow

geese and trumpeter swans that fly for a winter's
warm weather cruise

over a pond in North Carolina.
White feathers and off-white feathers, a

fluttering before your eyes
taking you to a world without any purples, blues.

You wanted to keep the baby. He didn't.
He wanted to keep the baby. You didn't.

Your pink warm-ups hide you as you drink lemon
tea in the big chair beside the television.

When your mother drives over with a yellow-
frosted birthday cake, you pull the throw

closer to the hill of your secret.
Too long you pretended the pool inside was a late

period. You floated on that water as if the baby
might swim away.

He wanted to keep the baby. You didn't.
You wanted to keep the baby. He didn't.

There on your arm is yesterday's
beginning bruise.

You bumped the door, you tell your mother.
Then you blow out the candles of your future.

New World

Cut edges of diamonds   rain in the gutter
your body a ship   the last oak timber

creaking   your cargo shifts in the storm   get
under the covers   they're wet

he's scared says he wants to go back to his dorm
not yet the baby is coming   alarum

as in Shakespeare you were on Depo-Provera
Lady MacBeth   Desdemona

remember confusion rising through tears
when you danced with Madison   the car's

sleek gliding as you drove past the mall
her feet pushing inside you   it's a small dark baby girl

when you run to the bathroom
she drops into the oval bowl   your womb

is a seething ocean
all your oceans are pain

and you can't feel your feet
have they walked to another planet?

she's breathing there on the towels
when you clean her   blood on the tiles

little breaths like a wind that turns lightly
a prayer wheel   a leaf that's about to fly

green towels for wrapping her gurgle
then her silence   the bathtub full

of your grief   you hold the back of her head, her arm
he says he has to take a math exam

Born

So she comes with her little gasps and flutters.
Never a cry. The moment you wrap her in a towel
and lay her on the tiles of the bathroom floor

she sees the light of your hair

where a universe begins expanding.
Small finger clutches as if she were pulling up grass
while inside her eyelids float the thousands and thousands of seas.

Your mind is sheep's wool and fog.
When you carry her through the glass door
and throw her into the dark of the dumpster

she has already memorized every cell in both your bodies
like the stars in two skies.

Genetics

A mouse has done this, and the common swallow,
lemur catta. Among the leaves and grasses
they kill their young to keep tomorrow.
A mouse has done this and the common swallow.
You wrap your child in fear and instinct, sorrow,
place her deep where sunlight never passes.
A mouse has done this, and the common swallow,
lemur catta among the leaves and grasses.

Hormones

The taste of tin in your mouth vanishes
like snow on a crocus.

Your endocrine glands are opening up new trails—
estrogen, progesterone, bundles

of oxytocin, placental lactogen.
It's as if you've forgotten

the baby already, her search
for your nipple, her fingers' touch

on your breast, a thumb,
a mouth poised for colostrum.

Everything is flooding and receding, your tears a
torrent, and all the time the placenta

is still inside you. Blood in the toilet bowl,
blood on your thighs, and one red towel.

Where did you put her—Star, Little Tigress?
Why can't you remember where she is?

Mostly

Most of all, you want the bleeding to stop
and to wear your bikini in Florida,
delicate shells curled on the beach
inside each one a trickle of white sand,
sigh of palm trees over your head,
over your whole body the water in the pool spreading
nuances of blue and green and golden light.

Mostly you want to board Flight 387 with your father to
another world. You push the bikini's yellow stripes
down in the canvas bag, a tank top, shorts, as
if the clots weren't flowing deep
scarlet, your legs two riverbeds for streams
of what's still in you, where the baby
nestled all those months.

Mostly now, you want your lover to come back
and hold you, drive you, wrap you all in white.
Dream you didn't throw her to the dark. But
interns push your abdomen, a nurse waits
silently for what's to come. It feels like a fish
on a dock, sliding down the planks.
Nothing you tell the police makes any sense.

Strawberry Festival

It's hard to drag, this big sack of what you should have done.
                                                        —William Stafford

Your mother wears white linen,
brings you angel food and strawberries,
whipped cream over the top like every summer.

You're thinking how you could have placed her on a step.
You're wondering if a basket may have waited for your baby's
floating in a grassy river.

Or if some kind adopting couple might have written
the story of her life, a skein of sunny days
knitted to make her

years from now a sweet, unguessing woman.
You never dreamed of judges, courts, attorneys.
You never dreamed of murder.

He moves across the far sea of the lawn
to take your hand, gives it a gentle squeeze
to show he's still your Pastor.

Hiroshima was bombed long before you were born.
On the stone wall of the Sumitomo Bank somebody's
shape is etched by violent light.

You have become that figure.

Under Pisces

What do you pack when you leave for prison?
Outside your window snow piles higher on

the branches of the plum tree as in April
white petals will drift among the swell

of twigs like lovers with their tongues to the sun's
melting sky. You will not be anyone's.

Can you take your favorite bra?
Lace, satin, underwire adrift among bikini

panties? That shadow on the window is yours
and someone else's where light hovers

but will never throw its net again. Your swimming pool
is empty as your uterus is now, a bowl, a shell.

Will an orange jumpsuit compliment your skin,
the rasp of heavy nylon

against others in the prison van recall
the baby's last small gurgle?

It must be a little like skydiving.
You can take only one tangible thing

with you, a parachute. And hope.
Then the whole earth starts to hurtle up

into your face: a lake, two rivers, hills around Bedford,
stones becoming larger, leaves unblurred.

They'll inspect your dufflebag for drugs, look in
your mouth, the cave of your vagina for a weapon.

Can you take your eiderdown pillow,
sweet as the skin of sorrow,

soft as the ghost that goes with you everywhere?

The Inmate Remembers

The scent of roses
through my bedroom window made
me turn in sleep
to give more of my body.
It wasn't possible,
full as I was of
his wilderness already.
I wandered along a path
in bare feet,
their whorls and runes
marking where I went as if
it could be some totally different place.

§

In New Jersey or Pennsylvania
someone is always hunting so
I had to keep my eyes
wide open (peeled, my grandmother
would say) when I was a kid
roaming the woods.
But from the corners where the lids meet
as in a kiss,
whenever I saw scarlet drop to snow
or fly to blue sky,
I never thought *cardinal*
but *that's what I want when I grow up.*
Flash and rapid, the sparkle everyone notices.

When the white wings of the amanita
unfurled from wet leaves where my feet
dug into the forest floor—
Death Angel—
I did not know those words.

§

Then I come to the Niagara River.
I lay my body down
in the current just above the falls
and let myself be swept
up to the edge,
go over the precipice,
plumage of peacocks, stars
in the water, collisions
of galaxies, atoms, animal eyes.
Who throws the white veil over me
making me a bride?
Who draws the white swirl of swords?
I come to the place where everything's
broken: bowls, timber, gutters,
kitchen sinks, a torn blue dress,
a piano and its threads of melody.
I can mend the song. I'll try.

Three

A Patagonia Calendar Cover

You're holding one
edge against the kitchen counter
as if the ridge of the mountain

were right there and you clutched a piton
ready for some crevasse. Crossing the glacier
before dawn

when the light is most golden
on Cerre Torre, your feet are bare
here on the kitchen

vinyl, the feel and slip of frozen
other-world-ness under
the yearning to tell what has flown.

Fred Beckey asked you back in nineteen-forty-one
to climb this peak with him, no matter
you didn't have the fare even if there'd been

a plane to Chile from Seattle then.
You didn't go. Maybe it was the war.
You plant your ice ax deep where the sun

strikes the photograph and lean
out against the rope, angled to the refrigerator,
while you drive another piton

into a niche of your lost destination.
You can't conceal your desire
to sleep in the ice cave, show me when

the dried apricots ease from frozen,
how you make tea from snow. You're
almost at the summit where you plan

the old ritual, you and Beckey, in the oxygen-
depleted air. Along with your
awe of such height you take a tin

of condoms, empty it into the southern
wind and leave a message way up there
inside: Fred Beckey and Wayne

Swift made a first ascent of Cerre Torre on
March 22, 1941. Except you never
set a crampon

into Cerre Torre's cold terrain,
your love's journey a star
whose light keeps its own

distance even
as you almost tip the bar stool over
showing me the summit's shine.

And now a vertical ravine
you never saw. Old winds blow your silver hair
as we toast each other with some French champagne.

Mementos

The sun blazed all the bottles behind the bar a supernova.
It was a summer evening at Toots Shors and I wore a
sleeveless dress the color of a bird in Venezuela.

My date saw Joe DiMaggio alone, swirling the ice
in his glass where he sat not thinking about the face
of Marilyn Monroe, whose name had yet to pierce

his ears, but maybe pondering the outfield hit his glove,
hand splayed inside, missed and let fly into the blue above.
And then his expletive.

My date knew everyone in New York. When I met Joltin' Joe,
the Yankees were ahead seven games but even so
I think he was worried about the stats. All I know

is how that famous hand felt in mine.
Is that why you came home from Las Vegas with a cocktail napkin
signed by Frank Sinatra *from Frank to Joan?*

Your effort in middle age to bestow on me another brush
with fame? Today I push
through all the drawers in the house, flurry of rubbish

out from all those years lying in thrall.
That lost memento will appear one day and recall
a slender me entranced as the crooner's Adam's apple

moved to the rhythm and timbre of his voice.
You were terrified, waiting at some Army Air Force base
in California, runways between rice

fields. They called it The Hump, the Burma Road
ahead of you, place from which few returned.
As if from any life anyone could.

Leaving Rio in the Rain

We stand on our separate decks as the lights
of Rio blossom in a misty rain.
I'm sipping vodka near the aqua of the pool.
This is how our lives will be from now on.
You are somewhere totally beyond my saving
while a thousand glowing flights of illumination
climb every hill around the harbor.
I want to go with you. They reflect in the water
where the ship leaves a scallop of wake as it leaves.
And again, lights in the air where each
shimmering drop is a kind of longing
to make descent beautiful, to wrap
whatever kills in tenderness.

About Your Eyes

I remember your eyes whenever I see Cape Coral
in the news, you staring through the windshield
at a sudden fuzziness.

I remember your eyes squinting at one ocean in the morning
and the other at noon and the cloud we passed through
on landing was the cloud you'd later live with.

My old World War II bomber pilot, I remember
letting you drive to the ophthalmologist alone in the cockpit
of your Mazda, but it was years

before the diagnosis of glaucoma
made you tremble as we sat in the blue plastic chairs
waiting to renew your drivers license.

Because you couldn't pass the test,
your eyes that night suddenly misted over
across the table from me at the Italian restaurant.

It was your birthday. A candle flame rose between us
bright and trembling.
Martinis. Salad. Linguine with a clam sauce.

You said you'd been driving for nearly seventy years.
You were wistful, looking back across that vista
of flat tires and shifting gears and heady rides

over mountain passes on black ice. Or the nights
you fumbled around in the dark of a parked car
with a girl whose face you almost remember.

Tonight, I'll put two drops in each of your eyes.
You'll blink looking up at the ceiling
where cirrus and cumulus drift on their sky routes

making you memorize again and again and too late
how to keep the car on the right side of the yellow line,
and how to steer through the next curve coming.

From the Deck

All that last summer the crows groomed each other
where they perched on the fiber optics line,
slender as fishing filament, carrier of many languages
like the crow. All that last summer

when it was warm enough, I tried to coax you
out onto the deck to look at the sunset,
the Sound in its satin cummerbunds
of many colors. But you refused to be dazzled

as I helped you over the threshold
because you were too weary.
You clung to my arm. It's okay. It's okay.
Just a small bump in the doorway.

I had the deck chair placed close by,
guiding you to it like that small boat
you once maneuvered into the inlet.
And you sat there three minutes, maybe five.

You were looking out to where you had been
with Vancouver, Juan de Fuca, Captain Cook.
Although your love was mountains
you brought a tin cup from your tent

and filled it with sea water.
You let it rest there in your eyes
those summer nights, taking a taste
of remembrance.

72

Then you wanted to come back in
like the crows
that caw their black goodnights across the sky.
What language will we speak afterward?

I Find Your Dry Fly Tying Gear

Dusty jars
lids that say Bernarden Mason
Skippy's Creamy
Peanut Butter
Kerr's Self-Sealing
labeled raptor,
bird fur
English hare's ear guard hairs.
A whole jar
bulging with sky
as if a flock of Lazuli buntings
were trapped in there.
A jar of rain:
saddle hackles,
bucktail
a deer can be so
many different shades
of baby hair
honey and roan,
brown horse hair,
cream coyote, grizzle
at the bottom wrapped
in something like a turkey neck.
The magnifier poises
its crane over
slender colors:
Dry Spruce Fly,
Pale Watery Dun,

Black Midge
so light
over the pale green
ripples of the river.
Tape curls on a jar
for peach preserves,
Primaries.
Smucker's jam jar: duck quill,
ring necked pheasant tail.
Below, a drawer full of
needle nose pliers
slender grasp
of neoprene thread
tying everything together
before you let each one go:
Light Variant
Adams Irresistable
Bird's Stone Fly

Sand, Rose Petals, Bones

I stand with my feet in the sand
beside the river, knowing the drought
has brought the two shores closer,

looking between my toes for withered
rose petals, for the white talcum
of your ashes so heavy I saw them drift and sink

like a scarf pulled down in a strong wind.
It was your wish,
this very river, this kind of strewing.

The fracture line between air and water
is only a furrow, always changing,
the plow of separation pulled by a single animal.

BIOGRAPHICAL NOTE

Joan Swift was born Joan Angevine and grew up in Rochester, New York, but has lived most of her life in the Seattle area of WashingtonState. She holds a B.A. from Duke and an M.A. in English-Creative Writing from the University of Washington. The last two of her four full-length books of poetry, *The Dark Path of Our Names* and *The Tiger Iris,* both won the Washington State Governors' Award. Among her prizes and other awards are three National Endowment for the Arts Creative Writing Fellowships, an Ingram Merrill Foundation Grant, awards from The Washington State Arts Commission, The Lucille Medwick Memorial Award from the Poetry Society of America, and a Pushcart Prize.

"this" = her whole email
to me when Laurie killed herself

CPSIA information can be obtained
at www.ICGtesting.com
Printed in the USA
LVOW08s1238040617
536884LV00005B/497/P

9 780692 862698